MW01128817

 UNIQUE
PUBLICATIONS

7011 SUNSET BLVD., HOLLYWOOD, CALIF. 90028-7597

DISCLAIMER

Please note that the publisher of this instructional book is NOT RESPONSIBLE in any manner whatsoever for any injury which may occur by reading and/or following the instructions herein.

It is essential that before following any of the activities, physical or otherwise, herein described, the reader or readers should first consult his or her physician for advice on whether or not the reader or readers should embark on the physical activity described herein. Since the physical activities described herein may be too sophisticated in nature, *it is essential that a physician be consulted.*

MFG. by DELTA LITHOGRAPH CO. VAN NUYS, CA.

TIBETAN KUNG-FU
The Way Of The Monk

BY MICHAEL P. STAPLES

■ *Acknowledgement* ■

The authors would like to extend their appreciation to Professor Wong-Lee-Foon and Mr. Jim Mah for their help with the construction of this text. And a special thanks to John Staples without whose help the book would have been impossible.

◼ *About The Authors* ◼

Master Chin-Dai-Wei (David Chin) began his training many years ago under the supervision of master Mah-Sek of the Fut-Gar (Buddha) Sil Lum style of Kung-Fu. He eventually became one of the only two official representatives in the United States of the Fut-Gar style. He learned Tai-Chi from master Kuo-Lien-Ying (one of the most respected Tai-Chi Sifus in the United States) and Pa-Kua (Dragon style) from a Taoist Priest named Yee. He then became the student of master Ng-Yim-Ming of the Hop-Gar, or Lama, style of Kung-Fu where he learned both Hop-Gar and the Internal Hsing-I styles. He is now the only official Hop-Gar representative in the United States.

Mike Staples began his training in Karate. Later, he took up the White Crane style of Kung-Fu. He is the author of the first book to be published on the White Crane style in the English language, which he wrote under the supervision of the vice-chairman of the White Crane Athletic Federation. He is a well-known writer in the martial arts, his articles having appeared in numerous magazines and martial arts publications both in the U.S. and overseas (Hong Kong). He became the student of master Chin and is now studying the Lama style under his supervision in San Francisco, California.

Contents

Chapter One

There were many reasons why traditional Chinese medicine played a prominent role in the historical eversion of Kung-Fu. Among these was the fact that the nature of the training itself was somewhat hazardous, but doctors scarce. It was impractical to depend upon a doctor who was a week's journey away. The result: masters of the Kung-Fu schools found it more expedient to perform their own medicine. A Kung-Fu oriented, specialized medicine therefore emerged.

The *Dit-da* doctors, as medicinally inclined Kung-Fu practitioners were sometimes referred to, weren't much interested in curing influenza or chicken-pox. They were specifically out to find better ways of treating bruises and broken bones in order to continue their training. Some astonishing medicines were discovered, most of which are well-kept secret recipes passed only to top students or family members of standing.

This type of medicine also found its way into other areas. It became prominent in the Chinese Opera, for instance, where Kung-Fu played an interesting and important role.

In the Chinese Opera, actors were required to perform many dangerous roles, portraying heroes of Chinese antiquity. The actors, well schooled in many aspects of Kung-Fu from an early age, invariably sustained injuries. Many Dit-da (bruise healing) medicines found their way into prominence with the opera crowd.

Shou-Hsing, the old man with a peach, represents immortality, the pursuit of the Taoist Priests. In his hand is a peach (sometimes called the demon's skull) from the magic tree, *Pan-Tao,* which blossoms only once in three thousand years, yielding fruit three thousand years later. It was this fruit which the Monkey King (an important figure in Kung-Fu mythology and the model for the Kung-Fu system of *Ta-Sheng-Chuan,* or Monkey boxing) was thrown out of heaven for stealing.

The medicine also became an outstanding feature among street vendors, along with many of the Kung-Fu styles. For instance, on the boat from Hong Kong to Macao, I recall an old man selling *Dit-Da-Jow* (Tieh-Da-Jyou in Mandarin, meaning the iron-hitting wine). He would draw attention to himself and his wares by beating his arms with a chain until thoroughly pulped. Then he would apply his medicine, demonstrating its curative value (or at least his faith in its curative value).

But another reason why Kung-Fu adepts were traditionally associated with Chinese medicine is that they were often doctors, herbalists, medicinally inclined Taoist priests, etc.

The Taoists who perpetuated Kung-Fu were interested in the art primarily as a vehicle to ride in the direction of their alchemical goals: immortality. Their alchemical research, turning their attention inward toward man's intrinsic energies, also turned them to Kung-Fu as a tool for unlocking these energies. It is difficult to separate Kung-Fu from traditional Chinese medicine (in the form of alchemy or herbs or acu-

An assortment of herbs, wines, pills, oils, resins and essences are used in training the body. They prevent the formation of callouses and arthritis and toughen the skin.

puncture) for on the one hand, Kung-Fu is a product of medicine and on the other, a method for its practice.

The ancient Taoist (and Buddhist, Tibetans and Indians) looked inward, to man's breath or Chi for the answer to both Kung-Fu and alchemy, strength and long life.

Chi was thought to flow through the body in a circulating way, mapped out in the various acupuncture charts. The elusive force surfaced, coming close to the skin, at certain points on the body and was manipulated by the stimulation of one sort or another, of these 800 or so points. Needles, as in acupuncture, pieces of burning herbs *(Ni)* as in moxabustion, or suction cups as in cupping, could be used to stimulate the sensitive area.

Chi was directly linked to the internal organs which were classified either Yin or Yang. The pathways or meridians, along which Chi was thought to flow, were also classified in this manner (a breakdown of which appears in *White Crane Gung-Fu*). The condition of a patient was, accordingly, diagnosed as being either yin or yang, depending upon the disease, and sickness arose when Chi was not flowing properly or when there was an imbalance in relation to yin/yang principles.

Since the onset of the recent vogue in acupuncture, much research has been done on the subject in both the United States and Russia (and France has been into acupuncture for years).

The meridians and acupuncture points have been replotted with Kirlian photography (an electro-photographic method of photographing energy fields) and have found that the film records disclose about eight hundred points on the skin where extra strong bursts of energy appear.

The ancient Taoist believed that breath, or Chi, traveled in specific routes throughout the body. This illustration is a map of such routes. Chi is drawn upon by Kung-Fu practitioners for strength and health.

Such an energy as Chi was considered so powerful, so ubiquitous in nature, the difference between sickness and health, weakness and strength, that if one could efficiently control it, he could accomplish almost anything. The absolute control of Chi brought the individual to superhuman levels of attainment. No longer bound to the mundane task of eating, he could live off strength drawn from the earth and the air he breathed. Subsisting on dew and moonbeams, he would no longer be sick, his energy left no room for disease. He was no longer subject to death's clutches for in him Chi was full. There was no room for fear, death or the enemy's spears or arrows. In short, he was immortal.

All this was but a part of the magic, inseparable from the cultural heritage of Kung-Fu. But without this heritage, Kung-Fu is no longer Kung-Fu. Without its cultural ideology, Kung-Fu becomes nothing more than a bunch of funny-looking movements, for you cannot separate the culture from the art without, as has been the case historically with any art form, wrenching it from its cultural heritage, eventually destroying it.

Traditional Medicine and Kung-Fu
We have almost no knowledge of the medicine of prehistoric China.

Cong-Fou. The Taoist practices called Cong-Fou were observed as early as the 17th Century by French missionary Pere Amiot. His observations were noted in a compilation now in the Bibliotheque Nationale in Paris. As Amiot noted, the primary reason Kung-Fu was perpetuated by the Priests was to aid them in their search for immortality.

We only have legends. Stories handed down from generation to generation.

Of the most important of these legends is the story of the three August rulers: Fu-Hsi, the author of the *I-Ching*, or *Book of Changes* (who developed the cosmological principles of yin and yang), Shen-Neng, the great classifier of herbs, and Huang-Ti, the purported father of Chinese medicine.

Legend tells of Shen-Neng, the Red Emperor (for his patron element was fire) and his glass bellybutton. His see-through stomach made possible the observation of the effects of each herb he ate. Setting out to classify all the herbs he could, and with the help of a god here and there, he managed to classify an enormous quantity of herbs before he died.

He was posthumously admitted into the realm of deities, becoming the patron saint of herbalists.

Of no less importance was Huant-Ti, the Yellow Emperor (for his patron element was the Earth). He was Shen-Neng's successor, the writer of the famous *Huang-Ti-Nei-Ching-Su-Wen* (or *Yellow Emperor's Classic of Internal Medicine*) which stood as the basis for Chinese native medicine for thousands of years.

The most common medicine Kung-Fu practitioners are likely to run into is the *Dit-da* medicine, used for everything from removing bruises to developing the tieh-sha-chang (Iron Palm). The medicine has innu-

The Red Emperor, Shen-Neng, is the patron saint of Herbalists. He is known as the great classifier of herbs. He tested and classified thousands of herbs by eating them and observing their function through his glass belly-button.

merable recipes and forms ranging from *Jyou* (wines), to *Yu* (oils), to *Wan* (pills). Its strength and consistency varies from that which can be taken internally to that which is so poisonous that it makes you woozy to stand next to it.

Another important and popular medicine is Ginseng.

There are five kinds of Ginseng, each affecting a different part of the internal anatomy.

The real Ginseng or *Ren-Shen,* affects the spleen, considered the center of life.

Ren-Shen (the man-shaped root) is a yang herb, increasing the yang energy in the body. It is like a super-vitamin.

Care must be taken with the Ginseng herb, for like anything used incorrectly, it can do more harm than good. For instance, because *Ren-Shen* increases the Yang forces within the body, a patient, sick with a Yin deficiency, will become worse with any increase of yang.

The *Sha-Shen,* on the other hand, affects the lungs. The *Hsu'an-Shen,* the kidneys, *Mon-Meng,* the liver and *Tan-Shen* the heart.

Ren-Shen has many levels of quality depending upon where it is grown, when it is picked, how it is aged, how it is stored and how it is

Huang-Ti, the Yellow Emperor, is regarded as the father of Chinese Medicine. Supposedly, he is the compiler of the *Huang-Ti-Nei-Ching* or *Yellow Emperor's Guide to Internal Medicine* which stood as the basis for Chinese folk medicine for thousands of years.

prepared. Its effects upon the user depend, naturally, upon the quality of the herb.

The cost of good Ginseng roots start at about $200.00 and climbs steadily up to around $5,000.00 a root.

Of the $5,000-a-root variety, there are only a few specimens, found in a couple of herbariums and museums in Europe. This may account for the lack of substantial research done on the plant.

Of the cheaper variety, the Korean White Ginseng and Chinese red and yellow roots run from around $5.00 to $50.00 a root.

The effects of Ginseng when correctly prepared, are varied. It may build wind, expel fear, prolong life, cure disease, invigorate the body or increase strength. It may do all of these things.

The herb is prepared by cooking in a special Ginseng pot or steamer for about six hours to make a collation which is then drunk.

Perhaps one of the most important aspects of the Ginseng treatment, and one completely overlooked by most Westerners, is the diet which goes hand in hand with the herb treatment. Any food eaten which is not a part of the strict diet will immediately nullify the herb's effects. So, if you are not following the diet and are wondering why the herb is

The Ginseng Pot, used to steam the Ginseng root into a broth.

Yang-Sum; a Ginseng root costing $500.00.

not affecting you properly, this is the reason.

Usually, the diet consists of not eating vegetables or fruits due to their counteracting effects. But this diet must be followed by yet another prescription which counters the effects of the diet itself for it tends to have adverse side effects (constipation). This seems complicated but is not all that bad considering you only have to take a good root once a year due to its potency.

Another common medicine is the *Hsiang-Yu* or fragrant oil such as *Bak-Fa-Yu* (White Flower Oil). This is often rubbed into the skin as an anti-spasmodic, or is taken internally (in small amounts) to clear the sinuses. Different *Essences* often come in this form. The *Essence* (Yao-Lu) is a preparation in which the ethereal part of the drug supposedly resides. Usually prepared by distillation, there are a great variety of essences, such as *Po-Ho-Lu* (Essence of peppermint), Plum-flower and White-flower Essences and even a *Dit-da* essence *(Tieh-da-yao-gin)*.

There are also a number of pill-masses, such as *Po-Jai* or *Ho-Ming-Sing,* which are groups of some 20 or 30 pills, taken all at once. Also, there are plasters (Kao) such as the popular *Kou-Pi-Kao,* or Dog-Skin plaster which is soft when warm and hard when cool, and powders (San) used both internally, such as *Sap-Ling-Tan,* and externally, for a variety of maladies.

Unfortunately, there is practically no way for one wishing to become familiar with the Chinese drugs and herbs to do so aside from finding a good teacher. Most books on the subject deal specifically with raw herbs, not preparations.

Chapter Two

Introduction

Footwork patterns are one of the most important and intriguing aspects of Lama Kung-Fu. They are heralded in fable and myth.

In a narrow sense they hold the secrets of the styles, philosophy and techniques. But in a broader sense, they hold the secrets of man and the universe.

Guiding the practitioner through movements which correspond to a unique and ancient understanding of man's psychic makeup, they become not only a means of expression but, by reacting with their maker, work an effect.

Very ancient magical effects lie hidden in the patterns, for they derive originally from the enclosed. The charmed circle. The magic of which has been preserved in countless folk customs not only in China and Tibet, but throughout the world.

The basis for the patterns reach so far back in human history that it touches up the deepest layers of man's collective unconscious, from a time when speech was of no substantial use.

Confucian Cosmology

"Such things cannot be thought up, but must grow again from the forgotten depths if they are to express the deepest insights of the spirit. Coming from these

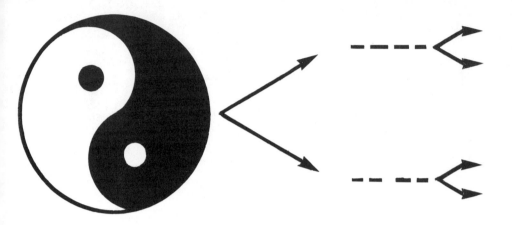

depths, they blend together the uniqueness of pres-
ent-day consciousness with the age-old past of life."
                                                    —C.G. Jung

The Tao comes from the void of the universe. The void, which has no margin, is extensive and empty, but from this emptiness, all things come.

Tao is established when mind comes into existence and the stuff of the universe becomes Tao's consequence. The Tao moves toward differentiation, producing opposites (yin and yang) in a coexisting interdependence, each necessary for the other's existence. Tao, then, is the principle which underlies yin and yang's existence.

Yin and yang represent the two primal, opposite forces; the full and the empty, the hard and the soft, the masculine and the feminine. The binary list is endless.

The generic term, yin, is often represented by a broken line — — ——, and yang, an unbroken line ———. Together they are known as the *Liang-I,* best represented in the Tai-Chi symbol.

The pugilist who understands the principles of the empty and the full has unlimited resources in the application of his techniques.

Movement and change being continual, the *Liang-I* itself moves toward further differentiation, giving rise to lesser and greater yin and yang:

From this division there emerges the quadripartite structure.

When dealing with direction, there are four cardinal points: North, South, East and West. When dividing the heavens, there are four divisions; the quadrant of the Dragon, the Warrior, the Bird and the White Tiger. When considering scholarly pursuits, there are four scholarly treasures: *Mo-bi-jr-yan* (ink, brush, paper, stone). And when dealing with the stuff of the universe, there are four basic elements: Fire, Water,

Metal and Wood. There is also a fifth—the Earth—considered an integral part of each and the central point from which they spring.

Each of the four yin-yang transmutations may represent a variety of things. But all divisions and representations are subject to a definite scheme. Because of this, they assume a specific pattern or order representing their place in the universe. Fire, for instance, is placed in the South, the seat of honor. Water is in the North, Metal in the West and Wood in the East.

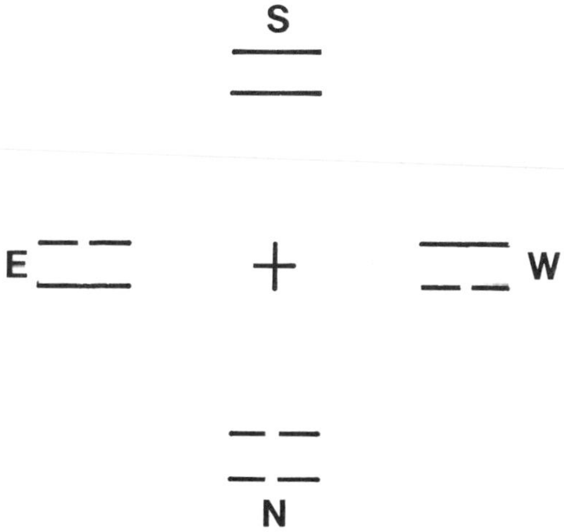

S

E + W

N

This, then, is the basic quadripartite structure which is represented in a variety of ways. Some illustrations are the Plum and Lotus flower patterns, the construction of stupas and pagodas. All complement this structure.

Both philosophically and technically, Kung-Fu also is subject to this structure. For instance, the style of *Hsing-I,* often called *Five Elements* boxing, is directly based upon the philosophical reactions of one element with another. It extends the structure of the basic pattern to encompass technique and psychological theory.

From the *Five Elements* arrangement, the next most important pattern, which is yet another transmutation of yin and yang, is represented by the Eight Petaled Lotus (also seen in the Christian Rose windows). This represents the halving of the elements. The result? The Eight trigrams or *Pa-Kua.*

As the Five elements became the basis of *Hsing-I* boxing, the Eight diagrams became the basis for *Eight-Diagrams* boxing or *Pa-Kua-Chuan.*

The original *Pa-Kua* arrangement, invented by the legendary Emperor Fu-Hsi thousands of years ago, became an extremely important philosophical symbol. It was one of the first symbols to represent the physical and psychological progression of events. It represents the seasons coming and going—the transformation of all things. In short, change.

When rearranged by King-Wen into a more philosophical, occult arrangement, it became the basis for one of the most important books of Chinese antiquity: the *Book of Changes* or *I-Ching.*

Just as *Hsing-I* was based on the quadripartite structure of the Five elements and *Pa-Kua* on the octagonal structure of the Eight trigrams, Tai-Chi boxing was based on the hexagram arrangements of the *I-Ching.*

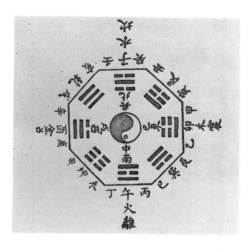

The hexagrams were simply the Eight *Kua*, tri-grams, doubled—or divided by half once again—to form 64 combinations. All 64 hexagrams and 8 tri-grams revert back, however, to the basic *four* structure of the Five elements.

The Tibetan Mandala

> *"Among my patients I have come across cases of women who did not draw Mandalas, but who danced them instead. In India this type is called Mandala Nrithya or Mandala dance, and the dance figures express the same meaning as the drawings. My patients can say very little about the meanings of the symbols but are fascinated by them and find them in some way or other expressive and effective with respect to their psychic condition."*
>
> —C.G. Jung

The Mandala structure is that of a flower, a cross or a wheel with a tendency toward the *four* pattern. As in the arrangement of the elements, the magic number is, again, four.

The Mandala creates a circle, a magic circle, to be found throughout both Eastern and Western worlds.

In the West, for instance, the early Middle Ages were rich in Christian Mandalas which depict Christ in the center with the four evangelists, or representatives, placed at the four cardinal points as were the five elements placed in their pattern. Another example of the ubiquitous Mandala structure is found in the ancient Egyptian god Horus with

his four sons portrayed in the same way. The Pueblo and Navajo Indians, also, used Mandala in their paintings. And the Mandala discovered in Rhodesia known as the Sun Wheel, dates back to the paleolithic period.

The Tibetan Mandala structure begins, as do the hexagrams and *Pa-Kua* patterns of the Chinese, with the movement and split of their concept of the original essence.

Tibetan *Vajrayana* Buddhism symbolizes the movement of Tao, or its equivalent, into two opposite forces the personifications of which are well depicted in the pre-Tibetan, Tantric Hindu deities *Shakti* and *Shiva*.

The Tantric Hindu text, *Kama-Kala-Vilasa,* explains the movement of the original essence toward differentiation, much the same as Tao splits into its yin-yang counterparts. Shiva, the Yang, active principle, stood contemplating himself at the beginning of time. Self-knowledge did not occur, however, until *Shakti,* the Yin principle, separated herself from him so that she could stand as a mirror in which his radiance could be reflected for him to see. Seeing himself he said, "I am," and his existence was realized.

Similar to the Chinese representation of the universe found in symbols like the *Tai-Chi* and *Pa-Kua* diagrams, the essence of the Tibetan philosophy is exhibited in symbols such as the *Vajrayana Mandala.* It is based upon one of the most common Buddhist emblems to be

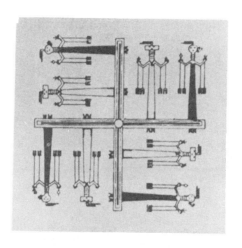

found: the Swastika.

The swastika is an abbreviation of the symbol which represents with the four dots, as do the flower and Mandala patterns, the four forces radiating from the central point. The arms of the swastika signify the four dots relation to both the center and each other.

The core of the Mandala is derived from the emblem thus:

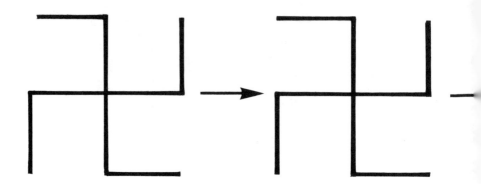

The format of the Mandala is taken directly from the pattern of the five points on the swastika, the four points and the center from which they spring. These five points are then replaced with personifications of energies, attitudes or psychological types constituting the theme of the specific Mandala.

It should be pointed out that the Chinese Five elements fit the pattern not only from a structural point of view but, also, from a philosophical point of view. The fundamental meaning behind Fire, Water, Wood, Metal and Earth is practically interchangeable with its Tibetan counterpart.

Keeping this in mind, it is pertinent to look at the basis of Lama footwork which is derived from the fabled *Muy-Fa-Jeong* of Ng-Muy.

Mg-Muy (a nun in a popular fable) drove a series of stumps, *Jeongs*, into the ground and practiced her footwork on top of them. A practitioner on top of the *Jeong* would have to adjust his steps to fit the distance between the stumps or suffer the consequences. Often, subsequent schools would place sharp stakes around the stumps to make the need for precision in stepping from *Jeong* to *Jeong* more apparent.

The basic structure from which the other footwork patterns in Lama are derived, such as the 13 star, 7 star, 4 directional, Pa-Kua-step, etc., consists of five stumps placed in what is called the *Single-flower* pattern:

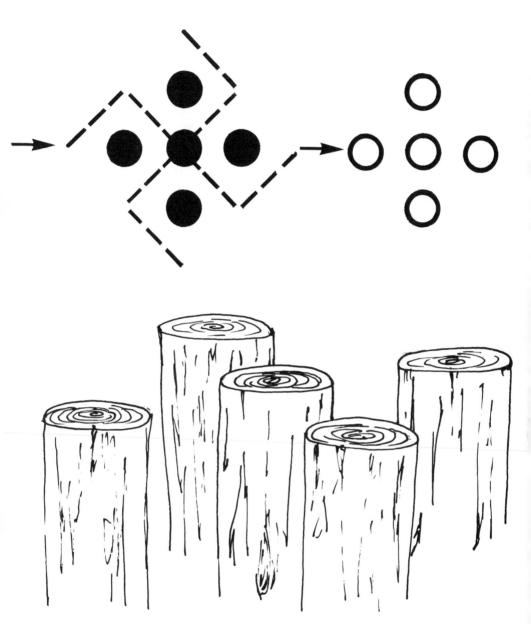

The *Muy-Fa-Jeong*

Lui-Lo-fu was a man of gigantic stature. His arms were like tree trunks and his body was hard as a rock. His Kung-Fu was exceptional, but his mind was filled only with thoughts of his own greatness.

One day Lo-fu set up a great stage in the middle of town with two scrolls placed on either supporting side which read in rhyme, "One punch can kill any Cantonese," and "Two kicks can kill anyone at all." He then sent out an open challenge to anyone who would dare fight, offering the equivalent of $500.00 to the man he could not beat.

Men came from all over the province to answer Lo-fu's challenge and to test his skill, but none could beat him.

As his victories multiplied, his audience became restive. Where was the successful challenger? Who could deflate this egotistical giant?

As their frustration increased, Lo-fu became more confident that his one punch could, in fact, lay low any Cantonese.

Feng-Tsai-yuk was the son of Mao-Chui-fa, who would beat her son unmercifully (for reasons peculiar to the fable). But Feng-Tsai-yuk, after being beaten by his mother, would steal off to the basement where his mother kept a large vat of Dit-da medicine she used in her Kung-Fu training. He would secretly immerse his entire body in it.

Over the years, Feng-Tsai-yuk's body, although himself still only a boy, became very hard. So hard, in fact, that he was practically indestructible, except for one spot at the base of his spine where, if hit, would cause his death.

When Tsai-yuk heard of the challenge issued by Lo-fu, and the statement that Lo-fu made concerning the Cantonese people, he became so enraged that he ran to town, jumped up on the stage and told Lo-fu he was ready to meet the challenge.

Lo-fu, seeing the youngster, laughed, but treated the challenge as any other, for it made no difference to him whether the challenger was a child, boy or man. Thereupon he shot across the stage and struck Tsai-yuk with all his might, trying to kill him.

Tsai-yuk, taking the blow, flew off the stage and landed on the ground, but was completely unhurt much to the surprise of Lo-fu who rubbed his eyes in disbelief.

Again Lo-fu charged the youngster, but this time Tsai-yuk was prepared. He had hidden a blade in the sole of his shoe and when Lo-fu got within range, he kicked up through his stomach and chest, ripping open his body. Lo-fu was dead and everyone cheered.

But later, when he told his mother what he had done, she became very worried. She knew that Lo-fu had a father-in-law whose Kung-Fu was very powerful, too powerful, she thought, for either her son or herself. They had better go to her teacher Ng-Muy at the Temple to ask for help.

At first, Ng-Muy refused to be bothered. But after some persuasion, decided to help.

"For one to best Lo-fu's father-in-law, his Kung-Fu must be very good," she said. "Every step must count."

Unfortunately, for the sake of the story, there is no reference at this point, that Ng-Muy built her Plum flower stumps as an ingenious ploy to trap the father-in-law of Lo-fu, however, as the tale continues, the father-in-law came looking for the killer of his relative. Ng-Muy answered the call.

The father-in-law thought he would have an easy time doing in the young nun with her round hat and fly wisk, and he was not put off when Ng-Muy cunningly tricked him into fighting atop her Plum flower stumps. Stumps or no stumps, he thought, how could the likes of a nun best his powerful Kung-Fu? That was a big mistake, for once he climbed up on top of the Jeong, Ng-Muy made short work of him.

The story of Ng-Muy's Plum flower stumps became very famous and the stumps became known as the Mui-Fa-Jeong.

It is from the basic Single flower pattern of the Mui-Fa-Jeong that many of the other patterns are derived.

The Walking-step:

(1) Assume the bow stance, left shoulder forward. (2) Turn your right toe slightly out and bring your left foot up next to it. (3) Step out with your left foot, pointing your toe out. (4) Without pausing in this position, continue stepping with your right foot. Move directly into the bow stance once again.

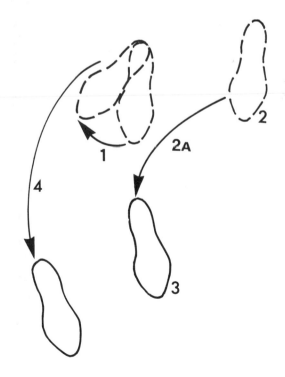

The Walking step in Lama enables you to better your angle in relation to your opponent without diminishing the strength of your own position. To face an opponent in the *negative* stance is considered dangerous. Figs. 71-73 show the reason why. This is called *bouncing out.* For this reason, when moving into a negative stance while walking, your foot should be stepping away from your opponent. The negative stance is considered to be a pass-through stance. Get into and out of it quickly to minimize the chance of your being *bounced-out.*

The Step-and-turn:

(1) Assume the bow stance, left shoulder forward. (2) Step to your right with your right foot as was done in the previous footwork pattern, but as soon as your right foot touches the floor, begin turning to the other side of your stance. Your left leg, now your bow leg, drags up after your right until you have once again assumed a locked, bow stance, this time with your right shoulder forward.

The Side-step:

This maneuver can be done either with the bow leg stepping (as shown) or with the arrow leg stepping.

(1) Assume a *positive* bow stance, left shoulder forward. (2) Step to your right side with your right foot, dragging your left up behind until you regain your bow stance after stepping.

BASIC PATTERNS OF MOVEMENT

Turning from side to side:

Before dealing directly with patterns, you must learn to turn from one side of your stance to the other.

With most of the stances, turning from side to side is fairly simple and self-explanatory. The bow stance, however, presents some problems.

(1) Assume a *positive* bow stance, left shoulder forward. (2) Keeping your eyes straight ahead, your head fairly rigid and level, begin turning to your left, shifting your weight onto your left leg. (3) Complete your turn by locking back into the bow stance, this time with your right shoulder forward.

When you have completed the turn, your feet should be parallel, your right leg straight and left leg bent. Your hips and shoulders should be turned as far as they will go and you should be looking over your right shoulder.

41

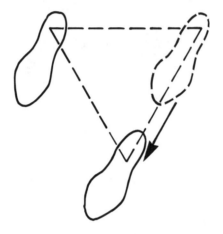

The Triangle-in step:
(1) Assume the bow stance, left shoulder forward. (2) Step in with your left foot, turning to the other side of your stance, locking back into the bow stance.

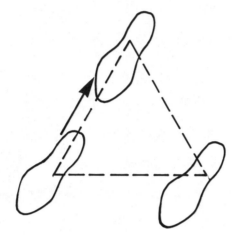

The Triangle-back step:
(1) Assume the bow stance, left shoulder forward. (2) Step back with your right foot, turning to the other side of your stance and locking back into a bow stance as shown.

The Walk-step-and-turn:

(1) Assume the bow stance, left shoulder forward. (2) Turn your right foot slightly out and bring your left up next to it. (3) Step again with your left foot, placing your weight onto it. (4) Bring your right foot up next to your left and without pausing, slide your right foot past

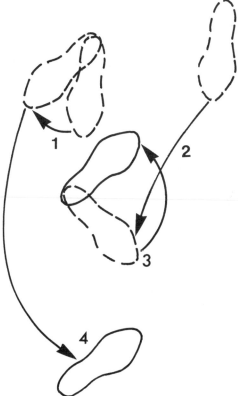

your left, stepping out. At the same time begin twisting to your left, locking into the bow stance, right shoulder forward.

▬ *Chapter Three* ▬

Most cats are curious and playful, often causing laughter but often causing a great deal of trouble for their mischievous activities. The great Lion who originated in Heaven, was no different. For years now Lion had been causing a stir. Deities came from all over the heavens to complain to the Jade Emperor who ruled over them. "This Lion is a menace," they would complain. "He is always getting into trouble, always playing where he shouldn't."

And this was not the first time Lion had been reported. As a matter of fact, the Jade Emperor couldn't remember himself when the first time was, and the Jade Emperor knows everything.

"Well, today he wouldn't get away with it," promised the Emperor. "Today will mark the end of that menace." And with that Look-Wong called Lion forth, chopped off his head and threw his pieces out of heaven, down to Earth to rot. "There," he thought, "that will be the end of that." And it would have been too, had not Kwan-Yin, Goddess of Mercy, been watching the entire proceedings from behind a silken cloud of mist. "Poor Lion," she thought, "doomed by his frisky nature. A bit playful, perhaps, but he never did any real harm. Maybe I can help." And with that, she flew from heaven, descending to Earth to help the undone Lion.

Finally, locating Lion where he had landed with a thump, falling to Earth, she tied his head back onto his body with an Enchanted Red Ribbon which she had brought with her. "The ribbon," she told Lion,

who was very pleased to have regained his head, "is enchanted. It will not only hold you together, but will also frighten away evil spirits, keeping you from harm." This made Lion very happy for he knew the power of the ribbon would keep him safe. Of course he had his own method for frightening away evil spirits, he had a mirror stuck in his forehead which would reflect the devil's image back for him to see, thereby scaring him off. But the ribbon was much more powerful.

Today, if you look, you will notice that every school's Lion is equipped with a mirror in his forehead and a red ribbon. And practically every Kung-Fu school, who can afford it, has a Lion for he is the very soul of the school. He is the flag, the banner, which in the old days, spoke of the school's martial ability. Schools would perform the Lion dance at festivals to demonstrate their Kung-Fu.

The head of the Lion is made of papier-mache and wood. It is elaborately painted and decorated with strings and fringes and tassels. Attached to its head, with a red ribbon, of course, is a long piece of colored silk, representing his body, under which the person playing the part of the Lion's tail must crouch.

This is the Southern Lion. The Northern, or Peking Lion, which is not quite so often seen, is actually a uniform the dancers must fit into (rather than a piece of cloth they crouch under).

Of the Southern Lions there are two types: the Old and the Young. The Old Lion is multicolored and has a long white beard. He usually serves as the trademark of an older, established school. The Young Lion, which is black, with a short fuzzy beard, is more often used by a school which doesn't have such a long standing in the community.

The Young Lion is very aggressive, always looking for a fight. He shakes with vitality whenever he meets an old lion and usually tries to provoke him. But the Old Lion is more docile.

Also, the Young, Black Lion often sports a multicolored bear show-

50

ing he is the meanest Lion around.

There are generally four parts making up the Lion dance; the head, the tail, the buddha and the drum or music section. The music section, in turn, is made up of drum, gong and cymbal.

Actually, the prestige positions in a Lion dance group are either the Lion's head or the drum. But the tail is undoubtedly one of the most difficult role to play for when operating the tail, the dancer must both follow the music and follow everything the head does. He is also required to crouch over in an uncomfortable position. For this reason, most people cast as tails are short while those operating heads are tall.

The drummer, also, has a difficult job. He must follow the lion with his beat and, if need be, adjust to any mistakes the Lion makes. He must be versatile.

Then there is the buddha head. The buddha plays a Chinese monk. The actors wears a pink mask (white if he's a she) over his head. He carries a fan made from a palm leaf. He plays with and teases the Lion, using a head of lettuce, called the Lion's *Chan* which the Lion tries to catch and eat. This denotes good luck.

The buddha is a very demanding, athletic role. Actors must perform like an acrobat, doing cartwheels and jumps and various Kung-Fu moves. The Lion, depending upon his mood, either plays with, bites or kicks the monk around.

There are two basic methods used in performing the Lion dance. The first is called the *free-style* method.

In this method, dancers improvise. They make the dance up as they go along. This is where the skill of the drummer plays an important part for he must match his music to the movements of the Lion.

This method is used primarily when performing in the streets. For example, on Chinese New Year's, the Lion traditionally prances through streets and back alleys going from door to door. He pays a visit

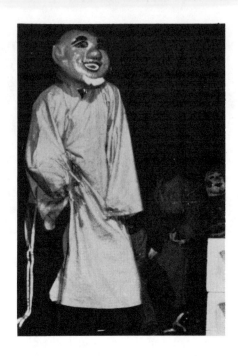

to stores and houses. The visit, called the *Pai* (which means to visit or to honor with one's presence) brings good luck. Those who are visited, put out a *Chan* which could be a piece of lettuce, or a role of money or a traditional puzzle.

When confronted with a puzzle, the Lion must know how to solve it. For instance, if there is a dish of water with some coins at its bottom, he must remove a certain number and leave a certain number in order

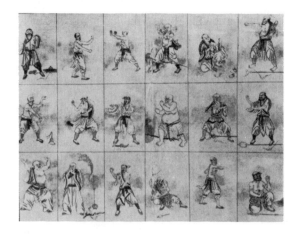

to fulfill the traditional act, bringing good luck. There is a long list of traditional problems the Lion must know how to answer correctly if he is to show the quality of his Kung-Fu school.

Also, there could be a problem such as an obstacle which someone may put out, to test the Lion's Kung-Fu. One which has no customary solution.

In ancient China, one Kung-Fu school might test the quality of another by testing their Lion. This would be a polite form of a challenge.

The school might, for instance, place the Lion's *Chan* at the top of a high pole or building and leave it up to the lion to figure out how to get it down. If the lion didn't think he could get it, he would pass it up. But this meant his Kung-Fu was not sufficient to meet the problem. There was a loss of face.

There was much prestige attributed to the Lion's ability in the old days. The Lions would even fight among themselves, one school's Lion against another. Sometimes, just to make it more difficult, they would fight on the *Muy-Fa-Jeong*. All of this just to prove ability of the school's Lion and, therefore, the quality of their Kung-Fu.

There was much competition between Lions and school in Old China, often ending in violence. Historically, Kung-Fu schools didn't get along. Even today most of the dancers, when they do go out into the street, stay more or less in their own territory.

Traditionally, one would not even leave the Kung-Fu school to begin with, without a sufficient number of people for backing in case of trouble. Usually, two people with *Tiger-forks* (Cha) walked in front of the Lion and two walked in back. The rest of the school brought up the rear.

Chapter Four

The Legend of the Eighteen Buddhas:

Once upon a time, many hundreds of years ago, there lived a very wealthy man in a part of China which was plagued with thieves and bandits. The man was known not only for his wealth, but for his kindness and goodness. He had maintained the standards and ethics of his day as best he could. Which was no easy task with all the bandits and thieves in his part of the country continually robbing whatever household they could.

Oddly enough, the man's most treasured possession was not one of gold or silver, but of flesh and blood. It was a large ox whom he loved and treated with the greatest of care. But this was no ordinary ox, for this beast (obviously the vehicle of some unknown deity) would speak.

One day, while the ox was lazily digesting a meal, a band of thieves stole into the barn and hid. They talked softly but clearly enough for the animal to hear. The ox recognized the thieves as being eighteen bandits who had been terrorizing the countryside for some time. They were easily recognized, for each carried a different weapon which he, it was said, specialized in.

The thieves ate, drank, boasted of their exploits, and laughed at their misdeeds. They eventually decided to rob their unsuspecting host that night at twelve o'clock, when he was asleep.

After the bandits left the barn, the ox immediately rushed to his

master to inform him of the plot. "What am I to do now?" said the wealthy man nervously. "I have neither guards nor strength enough to hold back eighteen robbers."

The ox paused for a moment (the way oxen do just before saying something important) and replied, "Throw them a party tonight and leave your fate in the hands of the gods."

The wealthy man, although aghast at the animal's reply, decided to follow his instructions, placing his faith in whichever deity it was who spoke through the beast.

He, therefore, had made a banquet with great varieties of food, drink, and lights, and put a sign over his door welcoming the thieves.

Midnight came and the eighteen thieves arrived to carry out their felonious plan. Needless to say, they were stunned by their reception.

Into the house they walked, confused and a bit frightened. They were met by their host who bade them sit down and eat, which they did.

Eventually, placated by food and drink, their confidence began to rise. They demanded to know how the wealthy man knew of their plans. They had told no one.

Of course the wealthy man spoke the truth when he retorted that it was his ox who had overheard them. But the bandits, at first amused, became angered. "This was obviously some type of foolish ploy to trick them," they counseled among themselves.

"Show us this talking ox of yours," demanded the leader of the thieves. "If he speaks, we will spare, but if he doesn't, we will kill you." And so, to the barn they went.

"Well?" said one of the bandits, standing in front of the ox, smiling sarcastically. "What have you to say for yourself, cow?" But the ox simply continued to chew his meal, ignoring his interrogator.

"Don't you have something you would like to say?" he went on.

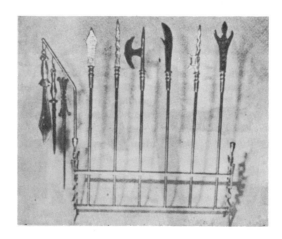

"Perhaps recite a poem or discuss the weather?" But the ox continued to chew.

"And now," said the thieves to the wealthy man who was shaking with fear, "you will pay us for your little joke." And with that they drew their knives and threatened the wealthy landowner. Suddenly, from the corner of the barn came a voice. . .

"You thieves are doomed for your evil deeds," said the ox. "You will be destroyed, and all die a merciless, terrible death shortly unless you change your ways."

The thieves were astounded and paralyzed with fright. They knelt down before the ox and, in quaking voices, inquired about their fate, pleading for mercy from the magic ox.

"There are two roads which you can follow," said the ox. "If you continue on in the manner you have you will come to a horrible end. But if you change, give back all the money you have stolen, and go up into the mountains to meditate and lead a peaceful life, the gods will make you all Lo-Han [Buddhas] ."

The thieves, taking heed, returned all their stolen goods and went up into the high mountains where they eventually became the eighteen Buddhas, fostering the symbolic eighteen weapons of classical China.

Weapons—The Tools of the Trade

Traditional Kung-Fu weapons of ancient China fall into three main categories (besides offensive and defensive which is more generalized still). These are the long weapons, such as spear, kwan-tao, and staff; the short weapons, such as knife, dagger and sword; and the weapons for throwing and shooting, such as coins, ball-bearings, darts or bow and arrows. There is also a category including a myriad of special weapons which defy classifications—hidden razors in shoes, magic flutes whose music drives the enemy insane, head swallowing devices, etc.

The men of Kung-Fu exhibited an unbelievable aptitude for creating new weapons to counter the opponent's new weapons. Wars have always produced counter-weapons.

The Chinese developed an arsenal of unusual devices and related war machinery probably unparalleled anywhere else in the world. There were hooks and blades under fingernails, swords and whips worn like belts, darts, axes, spears, clubs, smoking pipes, canes, benches, poisons and on and on. . . .

Historically, weapons were used for combat. They were a necessity— a survival measure. Like America's Old West, where almost everybody packed a gun, nearly everyone in old China, who could find the time and money, would study some form of martial art.

Although the age of dart throwing and sword toting is past, the place for weapons in Kung-Fu training remains, for they are an important part of the art, used to gain an understanding of what Kung-Fu is really all about.

From a technical standpoint, the Kung-Fu weapons are looked upon as tools for developing specific qualities. For instance, the Kwan-Tao develops strength in the arms and wrists, the three-section Staff develops timing and control, the sword grace and poise, etc. This is not to suggest that weapons training has no direct pragmatic application other than that of serving as a prop for the underscoring of an exercise (although in Mainland China that is precisely what the weapons are considered to be. The warlike value of Kung-Fu has been deemphasized with only its health maintenance and esthetic properties being retained.)

The pragmatic, technical use of the weapon itself is often not as important as the metaphorical training—the idea behind the tool or machine. This is something that isn't very well understood in the West, for

Westerners have a tendency to find great value in those things which are machine-like. They become absorbed in the practical aspects of kicking and punching, discarding the philosophical purpose behind the techniques. But, it is not the specific technique or tool which is important, it is the kind of parallelactic understanding gained from the principles behind the technique. Accordingly, to a musician, although he loves a good piano, it's the music produced that's important. The piano is just the tool to get at the music. This upholds the theory that the greatest art has no form (from a technique standpoint) but the form is always there because the principles underlying the form are present.

The point of studying weapons, as was hinted at in the chapter on Mandala, is that the means one uses to achieve enlightenment is not important as long as one understands them for what they are. Weapons are a metaphor in the sense that they translate experience from one mode to another. Kung-Fu (as opposed to Wu Shu, or the technique of Kung-Fu) is also such a metaphor for it translates the experience of Wu Shu, the War art, into self-understanding.

Becoming attuned to the underlying principles of a weapon (much the same as becoming attuned to the underlying principles related to the metaphorical animal forms found throughout Kung-Fu ideology) frees one to apply those principles to other forms (machinery). You come to understand the principles of a broom or a chair as well as a staff or a knife. The lid of a garbage can may become your shield, a pencil or pen your dagger.

Although the discipline, the method, or the structure of technique seems binding at first, it is meant, ultimately, to serve by freeing the spirit, for what good comes from having free technique and an imprisoned spirit? It is much the same as a free-wheeling jazz musician, an analogy used by other martial artists in their attempt to rationalize their lack of formal technique. Both the musician and the martial artist are presented with the option of choosing action by reasoning through a series of principles which have, hopefully, become a part of his nature. Accordingly, both should take care not to lose the principles of their respective systems. They are the means through which one arrives at solutions. Solution to the myriad problems one studies Kung-Fu to solve.

In this chapter, only a few weapons will be discussed. The presentation of even a fraction of the numerous weapons of China would be an extremely arduous task, worthy of a separate book in itself. Here will be discussed a few of the more prominent, well-known weapons which have interesting stories associated with them.

The Chinese are some of the best storytellers in the world, especially when it comes to fairy tales. There are tales of ghosts and goblins, devils and sages. They have a unique flavor all their own. Perhaps because, unlike the skeptical, Western "grown-up" mind that places fantasy in the realm of children and fools, the Chinese have believed wholeheartedly in what we consider to be the make-believe world. The existence of ghost, for instance, was never a question in China. Magic, fortune telling, geomancing, etc., were a way of life, not of carnivals, and the presence of a magic sword, staff or talisman was unquestioned.

I remember one of my Sifu's becoming very serious one day when I expressed my desire to purchase a rather old sword I had seen. He was worried that I might acquire a *devil-sword* owned by someone who was evil. Such a purchase would result in my inheriting the bad luck of the former owner (in a karmic transfer). One test of the sword's purity, he said, was to point its tip down and see if it dripped blood. I did, and it didn't—but I passed up the buy just the same. Such beliefs are widespread and thoroughly ingrained in the culture of China. They are expounded upon in the literature, theater, opera, and more recently in the misunderstood Chinese movies which have become so popular in the United States. These Kung-Fu movies, which Westerners predictably scorn as "unrealistic," portray legends, stories and feats handed down through the ages which are a part of both the Chinese culture and Kung-Fu. They deal with traditional folklore in which Kung-Fu had an enormous influence. And because of this influence, this book would be incomplete without relating at least a few of the more prominent tales. Perhaps the most outstanding of these, and one which conveniently tells the story of a wonderful Kung-Fu staff, is the tale of the Monkey King.

The Staff

Many years ago on the mountain of Flowers and Fruit, in the country of Ao-Lai, there was a magic rock which over the years had become shaped like an egg. One day this egg-shaped rock, which had somehow become magically pregnant, cracked open, giving birth to a stone monkey—the Monkey King.

The stone monkey lived and played with the rest of the normal monkeys on the mountain until one day, after proving his courage by penetrating the Water Curtain Cave and finding a new home for the other monkeys, he was made King.

Eventually, the stone monkey became bored with his predicament as King and left the Water Curtain Cave in search of adventure and immortality which he finally found after many months of searching. He found it in the cave of the Slanting Moon and Three Stars, on the mountain of the Holy Terrace.

Monkey had spent a good deal of time traveling and searching for an immortal who could teach him the magic arts and was very pleased to find Subodhi, the patriarch in the Enchanted Cave. But it was only monkey's cleverness which gained him favor with Subodhi, for the sage, at first, refused to teach the impudent animal. Finally, however, monkey did learn his magic and became an immortal. He then returned to his Water Curtain cave to greet his monkey subjects, only to find that there was a terrible ogre called the Demon of Havoc, who was causing a great deal of trouble in his kingdom.

Using his magic, Monkey slew the demon. He had learned many tricks from his teacher, such as the art of taking a hair from his head and turning it into an army of small monkeys who would do his bidding.

Having slain the Demon, monkey took the ogre's huge sword and taught himself, and his subjects, to use it. But he was very unsatisfied with the weapon. He decided, therefore, to go in search of a more suita-

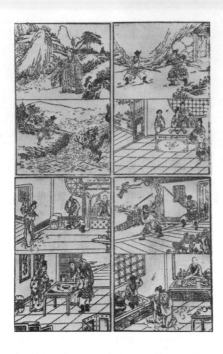

ble weapon, one which felt thoroughly comfortable in his paws. He thereupon decided to pay a visit to the Dragon King of the Easter sea, whom he had heard kept many magic weapons in his treasury. Monkey dove to the bottom of the ocean where he was greeted by this fishy Deity. The Dragon King first brought out a huge sword which monkey immediately scorned. Then he offered a nine-pronged fork weighing three thousand six hundred pounds, but it didn't fit monkey's hand and was a bit too light. Next, a halberd weighing seven thousand two hundred pounds—still too light. The Dragon King was perplexed, he had nothing left to offer.

At this point the Dragon mother reminded the King of the magic iron which was used to pound the bed of the Milky Way flat. The Dragon King replied that it was of no use, and was entirely too heavy to move. If monkey insisted upon seeing, he would have to go there himself. He did.

The piece of metal turned out to be a thick iron pillar about twenty feet long, which monkey took in his hands and raised. "A bit too long, I think!" he said, and the pillar suddenly became several feet shorter and smaller. "A bit smaller still," he said, and again it shrank. Monkey was delighted with the magic iron staff which he carried from then on in the form of a needle placed carefully behind his ear. Whenever he needed his staff, he would take it from behind his ear and, muttering a magic spell, would make his weapon as large or small as he desired.

This is a brief account of a part of the story of Monkey which is very

long. The magic staff became monkey's trademark. He is always pictured as carrying it when painted or carved by Chinese artists.

The Monkey King is only one figure in Chinese history, famous for his use of the staff. He is, however, a particularly colorful one.

Originally, the staff was supposed to have substituted another weapon such as a spear or halberd. It was used primarily by monks, as many religious sects scorned the use of strictly military implements such as spears. They preferred the more peaceful looking staff. It is a weapon, the use of which the monks of the Shao-Lin Temple were especially well known.

The Kwan-Tao

One of the most famous personalities of ancient China is Kwan-Kung, to whom some 1,600 Temples were erected throughout the country. Kwan-Kung is worshiped as the Deity of War.

A General during the later Han dynasty, Kwan-Kung rose from poverty to become one of the most hallowed military figures in Chinese history and was later immortalized in the novel called *Romance of the Three Kingdoms.*

Kwan-Kung was a native of Chieh-Liang in the Shansi province of China. But he was forced to flee his home and live the life of a wandering criminal after slaying an official who was tormenting one of his friends. Eventually Kwan joined with two comrades: Liu-Pei and Chang-Fei, and the three of them became known as the Three Brothers of the Peach Orchard.

The Three Brothers, attempting to unite the then troubled Chinese Empire began a crusade which catapulted them into the ranks of great men of Chinese history. Especially well known and loved, however, was Kwan-Kung who became a Robin Hood type figure, fighting for the oppressed and downtrodden with his infamous Kwan-Tao, the large halberd named after the famous general.

Kwan-Kung became the patron Saint of the martial arts. His picture can usually be found in training halls. Although Kwan represents the epitome of righteousness, honesty, loyalty, etc., he was never much of a representative of peacefulness. He left quite an enormous trail of bodies in the wake of his travels, and for this reason some Kung-Fu schools, of a more peaceful nature, will not honor him as their patron saint.

When Kwan-Kung died, he died a warrior's death—in battle. His head was chopped off.

For many days after his death his spirit screamed, "Give me back my head!" driving everyone in the land crazy with fear. Finally, a Monk was summoned to help. He chastised Kwan's spirit for complaining so much at the loss of his single head after having killed so many. And with that, the screams subsided.

The Sword

The sword is known as the *mother* of weapons. Said to have been invented by Ch'ih Yu (an early mythical ruler in China) who forged the double-edged sword from gold which he found in the mountains, the sword, aside from its attributes as a weapon possessed of supernatural qualities (used to chase away evil demons—note the coin sword which is hung over one's bed to scare away ghosts) was perhaps one of the most important emblems of ancient China. It was reserved for the upper-class, and was the mark of kings and high officials who carried it as a badge of rank. The sword symbolizes wisdom, power and magic and is the emblem of the sage.

Famous for his sword is Lu-Tung-Pin, one of the *eight immortals,* who owned a magic sword. Lu would hold the scabbard of his weapon and the blade would jump from its sheath to obey his commands.

Lu-Tung-Pin was originally a governor of one of the states of China but became disenchanted with his station in life when confronted time and time again with the people's squabbles and wards, so prevalent during his time. He, therefore, took his wife and child and left. Eventually, he left his wife and child too, preferring the life of a recluse. He lived high atop a mountain where he studied Taoist philosophy and magic.

After many years of celebate studies and practice, Lu became aware of the secret of life and ascended to heaven as an immortal. His emblem, as mentioned before, was the sword, which his Sifu, Chung-Li-Chuan (another of the *eight immortals*—who carried an enchanted fan) taught him the secrets. Chung-Li-Chuan taught his pupil many sword tricks, including how to throw his weapon over 100 feet, to recall it so that it would return to its sheath when finished with its work.

But Lu-Tung-Pin never cherished killing. He was known for slaying only bad dragons, ghosts and evil demons. Also, he became the patron saint of barbers when he alone was able to shave the head of Emperor Chu-Hung-Wu. No one else was able to shave the Emperor without hurting him due to a scalp disease. Lu, changing his magic sword into a barber's razor, not only shaved the Emperor's head, but cured him of the disease as well.

The Spear

The spear is known as the *King* of weapons. There are many different kinds of spears, some for throwing, some for cavalry use and some for infantry use. It is probably one of the most ancient weapons in the Chinese arsenal, evolving from a simple pointed stick.

Spears fall into a number of categories which not only pertain to their use (e.g., defensive or offensive) but when they were developed. There was a particular type of spear used in the Han dynasty, for instance, another in the Shang dynasty, and so on. The early spear is one of the Wu-Ping or five weapons, invented by Ch'ih Yu. But the spear most well known, called Ch'iang, is said to have been invented by the Yellow Emperor, Huang-Ti.

One famous person known for his spear (as well as his sword) was the younger brother of Kwan-Kung named Chui-Wen (later known as Chui-Chi-Lung). He was a general about 1700 years ago who was placed in charge of protecting the King's wife and son.

Chui-Wen, who had gained an enormous reputation in his time as being one of the bravest fighters in the land, doubtless had many opportunities to prove himself and uphold his reputation. One such time occurred during the battle at Chang-P'an-Po where the Emperor found his enemy so powerful that he was forced to flee for his life. So complete was the Emperor's defeat at the battle that his retreat forced him to leave his wife and son in the midst of the enemy army. No one could save them now, he thought. But Chui-Wen (who, it is said, was born

from a star and had very special military powers) was determined to help. He was placed in charge of keeping the Queen and Prince safe, and keep them safe he intended to do.

In the midst of the enemy's attack, standing alone, in the middle of 10,000 soldiers, Chui-Wen made his way to the Queen, battling off attack after attack. Finally reaching the couple, he placed the young prince on his back, held the Queen close to him and began to fight his way back out of the enemy's arms. The enemy generals were, understandably, amazed to see the lone fighter in the midst of their army, not only withstanding their best, but actually pushing his way through, seemingly invincible. If swords would not stop this fighter, they thought, they had something that would. And with this the generals ordered their archers to open fire on the struggling Chui-Wen. Arrows from every direction sent up a black barrage of spiked wooden shafts, time and time again. But Chui-Wen swung his weapon with such skill that none could touch him. Finally, he managed to escape with his royal charges. The battle at Chang-P'an-Po was recorded in the annals of Chinese History as one of the greatest feats accomplished by Kwan-Kung's younger brother Chui-Chi-Lung.

The Knife

Unlike the sword, whose tip was its major strength, being used for thrusting and jabbing, the knife uses its blade to cut and slash its target.

One source considers the knife to be a descendant of the Da-Tao, or long-handled halberd (such as the one carried by Kwan-Kung). Another source (the Ku Shih K'ao—as described by E.T.C. Werner) ascribes the invention to Sui-Jean-Shih who made the weapon by melting gold. Another places its origin with the famous Emperor Chou-Muk-Wong, during the Chow dynasty.

As the story goes, the Emperor at the time of the Chow dynasty, had a son who was destined to become the successor to the Dragon throne upon his death. This successor was Chou-Muk-Wong. But Muk-Wong had to wait for quite a long time until finally laying claim to the great seat of power, for his father continued to reign for fifty years after his son's birth.

Muk-Wong, during this time of growing up as a young prince, became well known for his eight war horses which were the most beautiful in the land.

When fifty years old, Muk-Wong's father died and he inherited the throne. He reigned for fifty-five years until his death at one hundred five. While alive, Muk-Wong enjoyed traveling. It was on one of his trips, while traveling through the Shi-Kiang province, that a wealthy man presented him with a large sabre, as a gift, which would cut jade.

═══ *Chapter FIVE* ═══

Most styles of Kung-Fu rely upon a strong horse stance, for a variety of reasons pertaining to the foundations of the style. There are systems which use stances for purposes of health. The stance may improve posture, straighten the spine or align the internal organs for improved respiratory function. Other systems use horse stances to increase the grace and fluidity of their moves. Still others aim chiefly at developing strength specifically for fighting.

With many styles of Kung-Fu the horse stance is essential to the proper execution of the systems techniques. In the Tibetan Lama style, for instance, much of the strength of the hand techniques, not to mention the ability to move in the complex footwork patterns, depends upon the proper development of the stances. They serve as a primary link in a chain through which force is transmitted to the techniques. If this link is weak, all of the techniques are weak. But even the styles which do not depend heavily upon proper form and stance cannot deny the importance of strong legs. As a Western boxer will tell you, the first things to go out on a man in the ring is his legs.

In ancient China, the Priests of the Shao-lin Temple stood in horse stances for hours or days at a time in an attempt to both strengthen their stance and test their meditative abilities. Although the Lama style of Kung-Fu had nothing to do with the Shao-lin Temple, the proponents of the style had this idea in common with their Shao-lin colleagues for they too believed in a strong stance.

The Lama horse set is a series of static postures. Each stance should be held, in the beginning, for two minutes, building up to five-minute

intervals.

The hand positions are a valuable asset to the set. They help build portions of the arms and shoulders, and twist the body into the desired position.

The opening, and closing, positions of the Lama horse set make up the bow. Bows vary from style to style and often identify the system. The most common bow in Kung-Fu consists of placing the right fist against the left palm which carried political significance during the days of revolution in China. The hands resembled Yin and Yang, or Sun and Moon which when placed together made up the character for "Ming" (the dynasty preceding the Manchu's which underground organizations longed to restore).

The Lama style uses both palms pressed together in its bow (a Buddhist sign of peace, removed from the political connotations of the previously mentioned bow). Since Lama was not a part of the revolutionary movement (which included the Shao-lin Temple) but was actually on the "other-side" being the official martial art of the Emperor, the Ming bow is excluded from the style.

The Chi-ma, or horse-riding, stance is used in the first position. Your feet are placed slightly more than shoulders width apart, and parallel to one another. Your knees are pulled outward and your hips rolled under.

The second stance (fig. 2): Now twist to your left, bending in on

3

4

your left leg, and straightening your right. Your hips should be locked and shoulders turned as far as they will go.

This stance is called a bow-and-arrow stance and is common to most styles of Kung-Fu. It is a very strong position favored by the Southern styles which rely on a great deal of strength. The name of the horse changes with the direction in which it is used (in relation to the opponent). When facing an opponent over the "bow" leg, which is bent, it is called the bow-and-arrow. This is the direction most Kung-Fu styles use. When facing the opponent over your "arrow" leg, which is straight, the stance is called the back-bow stance. And when facing the opponent to the side, it is called the forty-five degree horse (although it is known by other names as well). Lama is the only system which actually uses this horse as a fighting stance.

The third stance (fig. 3): By shifting your weight onto your rear leg you now pull back into the "hang" stance.

Variations of this stance are seen in most styles. In the "cat" stance or the "single-flower" stance, the details vary. Sometimes the forward (bent) knee is pulled out while the rear knee, in. Sometimes just the opposite, depending upon the style. In the Lama stance the knee is

5

6

7

pulled in toward the rear leg and the heel of the forward foot is turned slightly out.

Praying Mantis or Karate, or Choy-Li-Fut have similar stances, but the details vary so that each style's respective "hang" stance looks slightly different.

The fourth stance (fig. 4): Twisting clockwise, you now bring your knee up behind your left leg until it touches your calf. Place the majority of weight on your forward leg, and twist your shoulders and hips as far counterclockwise as possible.

This is another stance which is known by many names. Sometimes called the Tiger-step, or the female stance: *Nui-ma*, after the character for female which bears some resemblance to the position. It is also known by a variety of names within the Lama system that vary with the manner in which the horse is moved into. One can move into the stance by stepping forward, across your front leg, by stepping backward, crossing your rear leg, or by simply twisting. Therefore the position may be called the "cross-over" stance or the "twisting-horse."

The fifth stance (fig. 5): Rise up on your leg (left), raising your right knee as high as it will go, and point your right toe toward your left kneecap. Called the "Crane" stance in some styles, Lama calls this

position the "Single-leg" stance. It is primarily a defensive maneuver used to retract the leg from danger. It can be used to withdraw the leg from a low sweep or kick, or can be used to block a variety of kicks. There is even a maneuver in the Law-horn subsystem which makes up Lama Kung-Fu, used as a locking maneuver to tie the opponent up.

The sixth stance (fig. 6): The back-bow stance is essentially the same as the bow-and-arrow, except that you are looking over your "arrow" leg (the straight leg—in this case your left) rather than your "bow" leg. Make sure that your hips are locked and your legs pinched in at the thigh.

The seventh stance (fig. 7): Dropping down on your "bow" leg you now move into the "single-splits" stance as shown. Keep your left leg straight and both feet flat on the floor.

This is a unique stance which is greatly underestimated. It can be used both offensively and defensively to retreat or attack. It can be used to drop under a high kick or as a setup for another technique. A few styles have a large number of techniques devoted to "close-to-the-ground" maneuvers, but the single-splits (also called the shovel, or sweep position) is common to most styles—at least in appearance if not in use.

The eighth stance (fig. 8): By shifting your weight onto your left leg, you draw your right knee up close to it (until they touch) and place the majority of your weight on the left leg.

The ninth stance (fig. 9): Stepping out slightly with your left foot, you now move into the kneeling stance. Your weight should be evenly distributed over both feet, with your right knee about two inches off the floor. Your knees should be pulled away from each other.

The tenth stance (fig. 10): Now pull your left leg up toward your right, moving into the "cross" stance (another position unique to the Lama style). Place 60% of your weight onto your right leg, 40% onto your left. In this position you should pay close attention to pinching your legs in tightly at the thighs.

The eleventh stance (fig. 11): By stepping out with your left foot, you move back into the position shown in figure 8. This time, however, you use the toc-sao, or crane hand position, which turns your upper torso in a slightly different direction and, therefore, changes the horse slightly.

The twelfth stance (fig. 12): Drop down into the position shown in figure 12, called the "butterfly" stance. This position is used primarily as a limbering-up exercise.

The thirteenth stance (fig. 13): By crossing your legs behind you, you move into the "Kwan-Yin" stance which is meant to be a locking maneuver to tie up an opponent's leg.

The fourteenth stance (fig. 14): Finally, jumping back up into the horse-riding position, press your palms together, ending the set with the Lama bow explained earlier.

Glossary

Aikido: The way of the meeting of the spirit.

Bodhidarma: (Chinese Ta-Mo) The Zen or Chan Buddhist Patriarch who, according to myth, was the founder of Shao-Lin Kung-Fu.

Chan: In religion; Zen Buddhism. Also, a head of lettuce or role of money in the Lion dance.

Chang-Chuan: Long Boxing. Applicable to those Kung-Fu styles using the long-arm techniques such as Tai-Chi. On the Mainland, Chang-Chuan is used as a blanket term for a variety of styles.

Chi: Breath. Wind. The vital force within all things. "To listen by one's ears is not as good as to listen with one's mind. To listen with one's mind is not as good as to listen with one's Chi. What the ear hears is what actually happens, what the mind hears is what has not happened but remains in the mind. What the Chi hears is intuitional, coming from the depths of one's nature."

Chien: Cantonese; Gim, meaning sword.

Chi-Kung: The skillful manipulation of Chi.

Chi-Ma: The Horse riding stance.

Chin-na: The Grabbing hand. A specialized set of techniques for restraining or clawing.

Choy-Ga: A basic southern style of Kung-Fu.

Choy-Li-Fut: A combination of the style Choy-Ga, Li-Ga, and Fut-Ga. This is a hybrid southern style emphasizing long arm techniques.

Chuan: Cantonese; Kuen, meaning fist. A system of boxing (e.g., Hung-Kuen, Lama Kuen).

Chuan-Fa: The way of the fist. A generic term, such as Kung-Fu, used for all martial arts but especially applicable to the Kenpos style which is a conglomeration of a variety of techniques originally supposed to have stemmed from the Shao-Lin Temple in Fukein province.

Chuan-Shu: The Art of the fist (equivalent to Kung-Fu).

Tieh-Da-Jyou: Cantonese; Dit-Da-Jow, meaning the Iron-Hitting-Wine.

Fut-Ga: The Buddha style of Kung-Fu, originally from the Sil-Lum Temple.

Jya: Cantonese; Ga or Gar meaning family.

Gwo-Chi: The national Skill (equivalent to Kung-Fu).

Hop-Gar: Kung-Fu style named after the Hop family. This was the name given to the Lama style of Kung-Fu by Si-Jou Wong Yan-Lum.

Hsing-I: Mind form boxing. A boxing style based on the five elements, very philosophical in nature.

Hu-Kou: The Tiger's mouth. The space between the thumb and index finger.

Hu-Hok Pai: The Tiger-Crane system of Kung-Fu.

Hung-Ga: The Kung-Fu of the Hung family. Hung was the surname taken by the five ancestors when they escaped from the Shao Lin Temple upon its destruction by the royal guards. Hence the Hung-Men-Hui or Hung League, also known as the Triad society.

Hung-Sing: A style of Choy-Li-Fut.

I-Chin-Ching: The Muscle chang classic-book written by Ta-Mo.

Kwan-Kung. A famous General during the time of the Three Kingdoms. Kwan-Kung, whose portrait is often found hanging in Kung-Fu schools, is often referred to as the god of war. His picture, however, does not signify peace and is therefore frowned upon by many schools. Kwan-Kung murdered many people when he was alive. When he died, his head was chopped off and his spirit screamed for days until a Monk was finally able to scare him off.

Kwan-Tao: Cantonese; Gwan-do, a large broadsword named after Kwan-Kung who was famous for its use.

Lama Pai: The Kung-Fu style of the Lama Priests in Tibet.

Liang-I: The two primal forces (yin and yang). Also, Liang-I Chuan; the Two Instruments Boxing.

Li-Ga: The Kung-Fu style of the Li family.

Liu Ga: One of the five basic southern styles of Kung-Fu.

Liu-Ho-Pa-Fa: Cantonese; Look-Hop-Pat-Fat, the Six laws, eight methods boxing.

Mahayana: The school of Buddhism prevalent in all Buddhist countries except Burma, Cambodia, Ceylon, Laos and Thailand.

Mandala: A drawing or pattern representing the Universe with a tendency toward quadreparitrite structure.

Mien-Chuan: A Kung-Fu style requiring a great amount of limberness, popular on the Mainland.

Mo-Ga: A basic southern style of Kung-Fu stressing kicking techniques.

Mook-Jeong: A Cantonese term for a wooden dummy or device used in the practice of Wing Chun Kung-Fu.

Muy-Fa-Jeong: The Plum Flower Stumps. A series of stumps placed in the ground upon which one practices a number of footwork patterns. Named for the famous Ming dynasty fighter Ng Mui.

Nei-Jya: Cantonese; Nui-Ga, the Internal style or family of Martial Arts.

Pa-Hsien: The Eight fairies (Immortals).

Pai: System, e.g., Lama Pai, Bak Hoc Pai, Tang Lang Pai.

Pak Hoc Pai: The White Crane style of Boxing, one of the methods of the Lama style.

Pa-Kua: The Eight Diagrams. A Secret Society. The Eight Tri-grams arrangement of Fu-Ki. An internal style of Kung-Fu.

Pa-Kua-Chang: The Pa-Kua Palm. There are a variety of palms used in Pa-Kua, the Ox-tongue palm, the Dragon-claw palm, etc.

Pat-Mei: The White Eyebrow style of Kung-Fu. Named after its originator, supposedly a Shao-Lin priest with White Eyebrows.

Ren-Shen: The man-shaped root—Ginseng.

Shao-Lin: Cantonese; Sil-Lum, meaning the little forest. The name of a Temple or series of Temples over the years in China.

Chiang: The spear—King of weapons.

Ta-Mo: Bodhidarma

Tam-Tui: Kung-Fu method stressing kicks.

Tang-Lang: The Praying Mantis style of Kung-Fu. There are a variety of styles of Praying Mantises such as Tai-Ching Tang-Lang or Seven-Stars Praying Mantis, etc.

Tan-Tien: A series of cavities (lower, middle and upper) where alchemical processes take place in the development of Chi-Kung.

Tantric: Used in this text to denote the Buddhism of Tibet.

Tao: The great Ultimate. All that has essence. Also, the way.

Ti-Sha-Shou: The devil's hand. Often, the Chin-na hand is referred to as such.

Tsao-Tsao: An infamous figure in Chinese history who would rather kill innocent people than risk the chance of harm to himself. It was during a head operation performed by Hua-To that Tsao-Tsao thought Hua-To might not like him and, perhaps, would let his surgeon's knife slip. Hua-To was immediately put to death.

Tsui-Pa-Hsien: The Kung-Fu system called the Eight Drunken Fairies.

Tui-Shou: Pushing hands practice in Tai-Chi.

Vajrayana: The vehicle of the thunderbolt. The term for Tibetan Buddhism.

Wu-Chin-Hsi: Book by Hua-To.

Wu-Shu: The War art. Official name for Kung-Fu on the Mainland.

Wai-Jya: The external systems of Kung-Fu.

Yang: The positive element in the Universe.

Yin: The Female element in the Universe.

Kung-Fu Ranking Systems

The Kung-Fu ranking systems traditionally follow the family system. Your teacher or Sifu is considered your father within the system.

Classification of older or younger are decided upon when you enter the school, not by actual age but by when you took on your new father. Therefore, a nine-year-old could be a 40-year-old's older brother or Si-Hing.

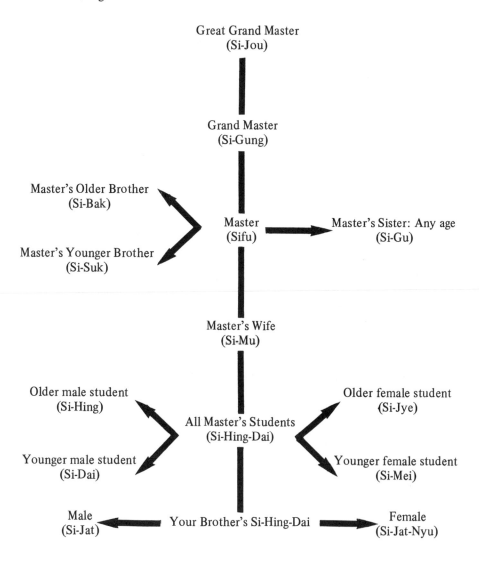

Great Grand Master
(Si-Jou)

Grand Master
(Si-Gung)

Master's Older Brother
(Si-Bak)

Master
(Sifu)

Master's Sister: Any age
(Si-Gu)

Master's Younger Brother
(Si-Suk)

Master's Wife
(Si-Mu)

Older male student
(Si-Hing)

All Master's Students
(Si-Hing-Dai)

Older female student
(Si-Jye)

Younger male student
(Si-Dai)

Younger female student
(Si-Mei)

Male
(Si-Jat)

Your Brother's Si-Hing-Dai

Female
(Si-Jat-Nyu)